中國探險家

Heroes and Role Models | Non-Fiction Series

Copyright © 2022 by Level Learning, INC. and Washington Yu Ying PCS™
Original and Edited Text Copyright © 2022 by Washington Yu Ying PCS™

All rights reserved. No part of this book in whole or part may be reproduced without written permission from the publisher.

Published by Level Learning, INC

Content Contributors:
Washington Yu Ying PCS™
Level Learning - Jingyao Qi

Illustrations by: Josh Taira

Leveling classification based on Level Learning standard.
For full description, visit www.levellearning.com

ISBN 978-1-64040-036-8
Traditional Chinese Edition

About Level Learning:

Level Learning provides a literacy focused curriculum specifically designed for K-12 Chinese as a Second Language classrooms. Our program offers 20 levels of specific and detailed objectives, leveled texts and passages, mastery-based online assessment, and analytics to enable data-driven instruction. Level Learning reading curriculum for both literature and informational text emphasize grammar and comprehension skills to help teachers develop confident and independent Chinese language readers. The non-fiction series of books are specifically designed to support our informational text course based on multiple national standards. To learn more about our entire offering, visit www.levellearning.com

About Washington Yu Ying PCS™:

Washington Yu Ying PCS is a Mandarin English dual language immersion International Baccalaureate (IB) World school. Yu Ying's mission is to inspire and prepare young people to create a better world by challenging them to reach their full potential in a nurturing Chinese/English educational environment. Yu Ying's comprehensive IB, dual immersion curriculum equips students with global competencies for success in the real world. As a leader in immersion education, Yu Ying is determined to advance Chinese language programs and global citizenry education by helping other schools create and strengthen their Chinese programs. For more information, email: products@washingtonyuying.org

很久以前，中國有一個探險家，他的名字叫鄭和。

鄭和帶很多人坐船去探險。

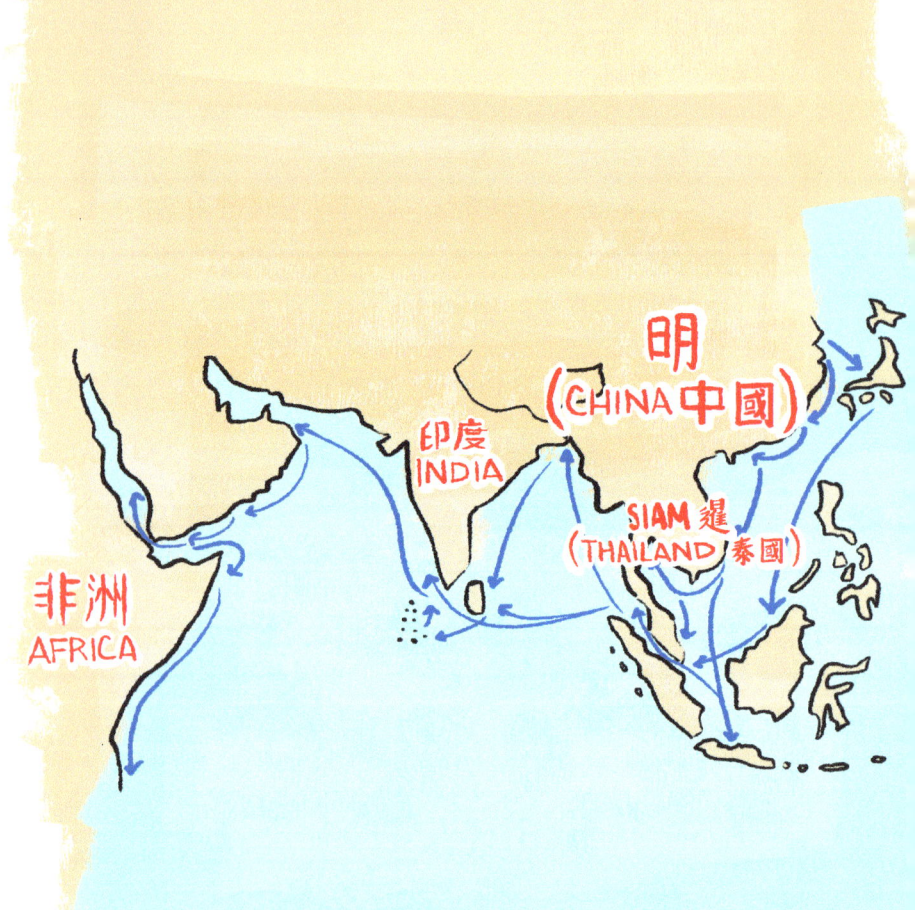

鄭和去了外國探險七次。他到了很多地方。

鄭和認識了很多外國的朋友。

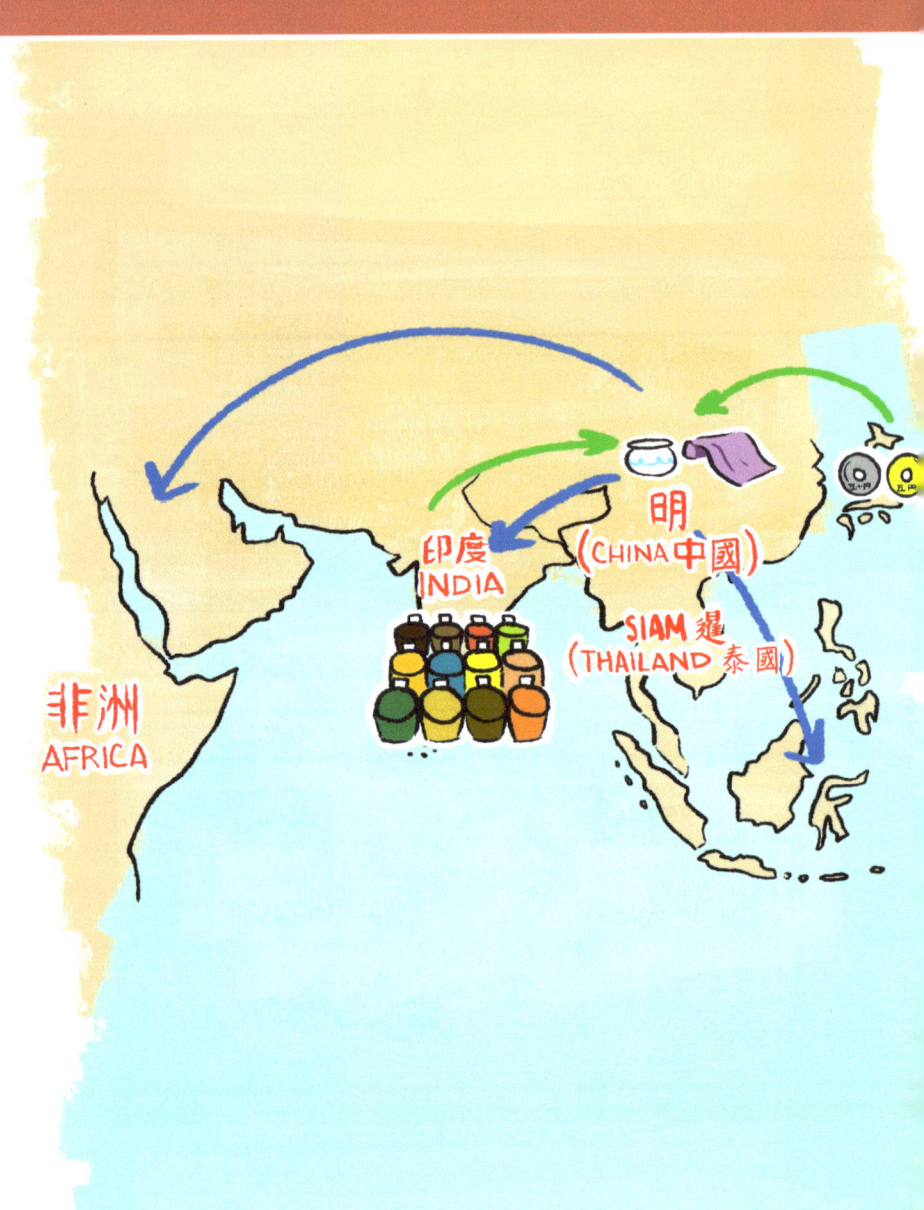

鄭和買了很多外國的東西。他也賣了很多中國的東西。

鄭和讓中國人知道了外國。鄭和也讓外國人知道了中國。

Glossary

	Pinyin	English Definition
很久以前	hěn jiǔ yǐ qián	long, long ago
探險家	tàn xiǎn jiā	explorer
船	chuán	ship
探險	tàn xiǎn	to explore
外國	wài guó	foreign country
認識	rèn shi	to meet
買	mǎi	to buy
賣	mài	to sell

www.ingramcontent.com/pod-product-compliance
Lightning Source LLC
Chambersburg PA
CBHW041226070526

44584CB00001B/121